W9-CDX-918

Dinosaurs Alive!
Iguanodon
and Other Plant-eating Dinosaurs

Jinny Johnson

Illustrated by Graham Rosewarne

Smart Apple Media

Published by Smart Apple Media
2140 Howard Drive West
North Mankato, MN 56003

Designed by Helen James
Edited by Mary-Jane Wilkins
Artwork by Graham Rosewarne

Photographs by
page 28 Science Photo Library
page 29 Mehau Kulyk/Science Photo Library

Printed in China

Library of Congress Cataloging-in-Publication Data

Johnson, Jinny.
Iguanodon and other plant-eating dinosaurs / by Jinny Johnson.
p. cm. – (Dinosaurs alive!)
Includes index.
ISBN 978-1-59920-067-5
1. Iguanodon—Juvenile literature. 2. Iguanodontidae—Juvenile literature.
3. Dinosaurs—Juvenile literature. I. Title.

QE862.O62J637 2007
567.914—dc22   2007005887

First Edition

9 8 7 6 5 4 3 2 1

Contents

A dinosaur's world

A dinosaur was a kind of reptile that lived millions of years ago. Dinosaurs lived long before there were people on Earth.

We know about dinosaurs because many of their bones and teeth have been discovered. Scientists called paleontologists (pay-lee-on-ta-loh-jists) learn a lot about the animals by studying these bones.

The first dinosaurs lived about 225 million years ago. They disappeared—became extinct—about 65 million years ago. Some scientists believe that birds are a type of dinosaur, so they say there are still dinosaurs living all around us!

Scutellosaurus

TRIASSIC

248 to 205 million years ago

Dinosaurs that lived at this time include:
Coelophysis, Eoraptor, Liliensternus, Plateosaurus,
Riojasaurus, Saltopus

EARLY JURASSIC

205 to 180 million years ago

Dinosaurs that lived at this time include:
Crylophosaurus, Dilophosaurus, Lesothosaurus,
Massospondylus, Scelidosaurus, Scutellosaurus

Lesothosaurus

LATE JURASSIC

180 to 144 million years ago

Dinosaurs that lived at this time include:
Allosaurus, Apatosaurus, Brachiosaurus,
Ornitholestes, Stegosaurus, Yangchuanosaurus

EARLY CRETACEOUS

144 to 98 million years ago

Dinosaurs that lived at this time include: Baryonyx,
Giganotosaurus, Iguanodon, Leaellynasaura,
Muttaburrasaurus, Nodosaurus, Sauropelta

LATE CRETACEOUS

98 to 65 million years ago

Dinosaurs that lived at this time include:
Ankylosaurus, Gallimimus, Maiasaura, Triceratops,
Tyrannosaurus, Velociraptor

Velociraptor

Iguanodon

In 1822, the iguanodon became one of the first dinosaurs ever to be discovered and named. Scientists thought the fossilized teeth looked like the teeth of a giant iguana lizard, so they named the dinosaur iguanodon.

IGUANODON

Group: ornithopods (iguanodonts)

Length: up to 33 feet (10 m)

Lived in: Europe, North America

When: Early Cretaceous, 140–110 million years ago

This is how you say
iguanodon:
ig-wah-noh-don

Huge iguanodon herds roamed the forests during the early Cretaceous period. They ate many kinds of plants that they chewed with their strong, flat teeth.

An iguanodon probably ate about 290 pounds (130 kg) of plants every day. That is like eating 150 heads of lettuce, 90 cucumbers, and 300 apples!

The iguanodon moved on all fours but may have stood on its back legs to eat or to scare off an enemy.

Inside an iguanodon

Big, strong bones supported the iguanodon's bulky body. The dinosaur had a long skull and a sharp beak at the front of its jaws for chopping plants.

Dinosaurs lived long before there were people on Earth. But here you can see how big a dinosaur would look next to a seven-year-old child.

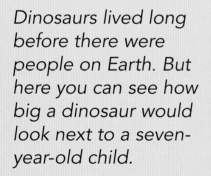

The iguanodon had unusual hands. It had a heavy spike on its thumb that it used to defend itself.

The three middle fingers were tipped with hooves, and the fifth finger could be folded across the hand so the dinosaur could easily pick up and hold food. No other kind of dinosaur had hands like this.

The iguanodon weighed about five and a half tons (5 t)—as much as an elephant.

When the dinosaur walked upright on two legs, its heavy tail helped balance the weight of the front of its body.

An iguanodon in action

Like all plant-eaters, the iguanodon was
often attacked by predatory dinosaurs.
It defended itself with its thumb spikes.

Most of the time the iguanodon
moved peacefully in herds as it
searched for plants to eat.

Living in herds helped protect younger,
weaker dinosaurs against attacks.
Iguanodons could probably move at
9 to 12 miles (15–20 km) per hour, running
at full speed. When threatened, an
iguanodon stood on its back legs and
jabbed its attacker with the sharp spike.

The iguanodon could use its thumb spike to kill an attacker, driving the spike deep into its flesh.

Ouranosaurus

This relative of the iguanodon was
a smaller dinosaur with a longer head.
It had two little bumps on its snout.

The ouranosaurus had a row of tall bones sticking
up from its backbone that was probably covered
with skin, so they looked like a sail. This may have
helped control its body temperature.

When the ouranosaurus wanted to warm up, it
turned the sail into the sun to heat up the blood
that flowed through the skin of the sail. To cool
down, it turned away from the sun.

This is how you say
ouranosaurus:
ooh-rah-noh-sore-us

OURANOSAURUS

Group: ornithopods (iguanodonts)

Length: up to 23 feet (7 m)

Lived in: West Africa

When: Early Cretaceous, 115–100 million years ago

An ouranosaurus's sail may have helped the dinosaur scare off enemies, or it might have attracted a mate.

Muttaburrasaurus

The muttaburrasaurus probably looked a lot like the iguanodon and had spikes on its thumbs. It had very strong jaws and sharp teeth for eating tough plants.

This dinosaur's snout was larger than the iguanodon's and had a big, bony bump on top. This may have helped make its calls louder. The dinosaur also had very big nostrils that might have given it a great sense of smell to help it find food.

This is how you say muttaburrasaurus:
mut-a-burra-sore-us

A loud call could be useful to warn other members of the herd that a predator was near.

MUTTABURRASAURUS

Group: ornithopods (iguanodonts)

Length: up to 23 feet (7 m)

Lived in: Australia

When: Early Cretaceous, 110–100 million years ago

15

Leaellynasaura

These small dinosaurs wandered the forests and ate plants that grew close to the ground, much like herds of deer do today. They walked upright but could scurry around on all fours when they were feeding.

The leaellynasaura lived in southern Australia, which was part of the Antarctic at that time. This area was not as cold as it is now, but winters would have been very cold and dark.

The leaellynasaura could probably run fast on its long, slender back legs.

LEAELLYNASAURA

Group: ornithopods (hypsilophodonts)

Length: up to 6.5 feet (2 m)

Lived in: Australia

When: Early Cretaceous, 115–110 million years ago

This is how you say
leaellynasaura:
lee-ell-ina-sore-a

Fossil bones show that the leaellynasaura had very large eyes that may have helped it see in the dim light of the Antarctic winter. In summer, it probably spent all day and night feeding so that it could build up fat to survive the winter.

Fabrosaurs

The fabrosaurs, such as the lesothosaurus and the scutellosaurus, were plant-eaters about the size of a fox or badger. They gathered plant food with their narrow jaws and sharp, pointed teeth, and may have lived in burrows underground.

This is how you say lesothosaurus:
le-so-toe-sore-us

LESOTHOSAURUS

Group: ornithopods (fabrosaurs)

Length: up to 3 feet (0.9 m)

Lived in: Africa

When: Early Jurassic, 213–200 million years ago

SCUTELLOSAURUS

Group: ornithopods (fabrosaurs)

Length: up to 4 feet (1.2 m)

Lived in: western North America

When: Early Jurassic, 205–202 million years ago

This is how you say scutellosaurus:
skoo-tel-oh-sore-us

These little plant-eaters probably did not live in herds like larger dinosaurs. Instead, they scurried around on their own, looking for food.

The fabrosaurs moved fast on their long, back legs. They did not have sharp claws to defend themselves, so they had to run away from predators. The scutellosaurus had bony plates covering its back that may have helped protect it from attackers.

Heterodontosaurus

This little dinosaur was a plant-eater, but it had unusual teeth. Unlike most other plant-eating dinosaurs, it had three kinds of teeth to use for different tasks.

The heterodontosaurus had sharp, pointed teeth at the front of its jaws. These were used for cutting leaves. Farther back were larger teeth for chewing. It also had two pairs of long teeth that looked like the teeth of a dog. This was very unusual for a plant-eating dinosaur.

Most likely, only the male heterodontosaurus had tusk-like teeth. These teeth may have been used to fight for mates during the breeding season.

HETERODONTOSAURUS

Group: ornithopods (heterodontosaurs)

Length: up to 4 feet (1.2 m)

Lived in: southern Africa

When: Early Jurassic, 205 million years ago

This is how you say heterodontosaurus: het-er-oh-dont-oh-sore-us

Maiasaura

The hadrosaurs, such as the maiasaura, were some of the most common dinosaurs during the Late Cretaceous period.

These dinosaurs are also called "duckbills" because they had a long, flat beak at the front of the mouth.

The maiasaura lived in herds. It probably walked on four legs when it was eating but could stand on two legs to flee from danger.

MAIASAURA

Group: ornithopods (hadrosaurs)

Length: up to 30 feet (9 m)

Lived in: North America

When: Late Cretaceous, 80–75 million years ago

The maiasaura chopped plants with its toothless beak and then chewed the plants using teeth farther back in its mouth. It had a very flexible neck, so it could bend and reach for food without moving around much.

This is how you say maiasaura:
my-ah-sore-ah

Good mother lizard

The name maiasaura means "good mother lizard."
Fossils have been found of the maiasaura's
nests, eggs, and young.

The maiasaura mother laid her eggs in layers inside
a hole in the ground. She covered each layer with
dirt and then covered the whole nest with more dirt
to hide the eggs from other dinosaurs.

Each egg was about seven inches
(18 cm) long—three times the size
of a chicken's egg! The mother
probably stayed by the nest
to protect the eggs.

*A dinosaur egg had a
tough, waterproof shell
to protect the growing
dinosaur inside.*

When the baby dinosaurs hatched from the eggs, they were about 12 inches (30 cm) long.

Their mother probably brought them food until they were big and strong enough to move with the herd and feed themselves.

Hadrosaurs took care of their young, bringing them food and guarding them from predators.

Crested duckbills

Many kinds of duckbill dinosaurs had a large crest on top of their heads.

Some crests were spikes, but the lambeosaurus had a rounded crest like a helmet. The parasaurolophus's crest was as long as the body of an adult person.

This is how you say lambeosaurus:
lam-bee-oh-sore-us

LAMBEOSAURUS

Group: ornithopods (hadrosaurs)

Length: up to 30 feet (9 m)

Lived in: Canada

When: Late Cretaceous, 76–74 million years ago

The crest was hollow inside and may have made the dinosaur's roaring call louder. The calls helped the duckbills in a herd keep in touch with each other and find mates.

Every type of duckbill had a different call and they could recognize the calls of their own kind.

PARASAUROLOPHUS

Group: ornithopods
(hadrosaurs)

Length: up to 36 feet (11 m)

Lived in: North America

When: Late Cretaceous,
76–74 million years ago

This is how you say
parasaurolophus:
pa-ra-saw-rol-off-us

Who discovered dinosaurs?

In 1822, a British doctor named Dr. Gideon Mantell and his wife, Mary, found some strange teeth as they walked in the country.

When he looked closely at the teeth, Dr. Mantell realized they were like reptile teeth. He thought they belonged to a giant iguana, which is a kind of lizard.

Twenty years later, a scientist named Richard Owen realized that these teeth, and other fossilized teeth and bones that had been found, belonged to a special group of reptiles. He called them dinosaurs, which means "terrible lizards."

Since then, the remains of dinosaurs have been found all over the world. We now know there were at least 700 different kinds.

Gideon Mantell was one of the first people to find dinosaur fossils.

An iguanodon skeleton in a museum in 1883. When the first iguanodon skeletons were put together, the thumb spike was placed on the dinosaur's nose, like a horn.

Words to know

Antarctica
The area around the South Pole.

Crest
A bony shape on a dinosaur's head.

Duckbill dinosaurs
Dinosaurs with a long, flattened beak, like the beak of a duck, at the front of the jaws. The lambeosaurus was a duckbill dinosaur.

Fabrosaur
A small, fast-moving dinosaur that ate plants. The lesothosaurus was a fabrosaur.

Fossils
Parts of an animal, such as bones and teeth, that have been preserved in rock for millions of years.

Iguana
A kind of lizard. Some iguanas grow up to six and a half feet (2 m) long.

Ornithopod
The ornithopods were a group of plant-eating dinosaurs that included iguanodonts, hadrosaurs, and fabrosaurs. They lived during the Jurassic and Cretaceous periods.

Paleontologist
A scientist who looks for and studies fossils to find out more about the creatures of the past.

Plates
Extra pieces of bone on the body of some dinosaurs.

Predator
An animal that hunts and kills other animals.

Reptile
An animal with a backbone and a dry, scaly body. Most reptiles lay eggs with leathery shells. Dinosaurs were reptiles. Today's reptiles include lizards, snakes, turtles, and crocodiles.

Sail
A structure on the back of some dinosaurs. The sail was made of tall bones sticking up from the dinosaur's back and was covered with skin.

Index

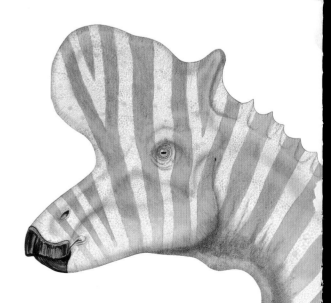